The Joy in Dying

*Restoring Love and Peace to the Dying
Process So Living Can Begin*

DR. T SKY, PhD

BALBOA
PRESS

A DIVISION OF HAY HOUSE

Balboa Press books may be ordered through booksellers or by contacting:

Balboa Press
A Division of Hay House
1663 Liberty Drive
Bloomington, IN 47403
www.balboapress.com
1 (877) 407-4847

Because of the dynamic nature of the Internet, any web addresses or links contained in this book may have changed since publication and may no longer be valid. The views expressed in this work are solely those of the author and do not necessarily reflect the views of the publisher, and the publisher hereby disclaims any responsibility for them.

The author of this book does not dispense medical advice or prescribe the use of any technique as a form of treatment for physical, emotional, or medical problems without the advice of a physician, either directly or indirectly. The intent of the author is only to offer information of a general nature to help you in your quest for emotional and spiritual well-being. In the event you use any of the information in this book for yourself, which is your constitutional right, the author and the publisher assume no responsibility for your actions.

Any people depicted in stock imagery provided by Thinkstock are models, and such images are being used for illustrative purposes only.
Certain stock imagery © Thinkstock.

Print information available on the last page.

ISBN: 978-1-5043-3634-5 (sc)
ISBN: 978-1-5043-3636-9 (hc)
ISBN: 978-1-5043-3635-2 (e)

Library of Congress Control Number: 2015910769

Balboa Press rev. date: 08/18/2015

Contents

Prelude

Neil: You need to go now, so I can go.
Me: Are you sure, I thought you wanted me
to hold your hand until the end so you
wouldn't be afraid and you wouldn't be alone.
Neil: You need to go so I can go!
Me: But you didn't want to be alone...
My voice trailed off into silence.
Me: You're not alone are you?
Neil: No I'm not. Please go now so I can go.
This is what we have been working for.

Slowly, I lifted my body filled with love, sorrow, and a deep reluctance from the recliner that had become my second home in the last ten days. I leaned forward, gently kissing my brother's forehead as I slipped my hand from his, knowing this would be the last time I would feel his touch. I made my way to the door, turning one last time to see his face. Sadness filled my body and my heart yet there was an amazing sense of joy as I saw him look off in the distance reaching for whomever or whatever was on the other side. Yes, I thought gratefully, there is joy in dying.

Introduction

I have thought long and hard about where to begin this book on finding joy in dying. I finally decided to begin in the place that was created for me through one of the most extraordinary experiences of my life, the place I discovered with the help of my brother, Neil, who was diagnosed with terminal cancer two years ago as I write this. It is through being with him during his dying process that I first gained the knowledge that joy exists in every circumstance in life, and death is no exception. I could not live the way I do now without having gone through dying with Neil the way I did then. Everything about the process of helping Neil transition from this earth has molded the person I am at this moment and the person I will continue to become. I have attended countless workshops and trainings and spent many hours in meditation, but the knowledge that I gathered from those experiences does not compare to what I learned about living in the ten days I spent with my brother as he prepared to leave this life. It is through joining him on his journey that I discovered what it takes to experience true joy and peace in living—and in dying. Although I can never repay my brother for this gift, I am attempting to pay it forward. So I will begin by simply saying: "Thank you, Neil. Here goes."

There was a time when the mere mention of death would have made me shudder and the idea of letting go of my loved ones would have filled my body with sadness, anxiety and fear. Most of us have or will experience that moment when we glimpse our own death: Maybe we were in an accident, suffered a horrible illness, or faced a situation that made us think, *I'm not going to make it out of this alive.* Maybe it was a time when we watched a loved one pass away or perhaps even the moment when our child was born, and we despaired of ever leaving him or her. There are many events in our life that offer us a preview of the transience of our human bodies and heighten awareness of our mortality. Those moments used to send chills through my body, and I must confess I have no desire to face my own death anytime soon. Yet when I contemplate dying now, instead of sending my body into emotional overload, a sense of calm and peace settles over me. This feeling of serenity is present when I think of my own dying process as well as that of others in my life whom I dearly love. This sense of tranquility was not present before.

It's important that you understand that I do not find joy in death and I do not have a wish for anyone in my life to die. Far from it. What I am advocating is that we live life to the fullest regardless of whether we have one day, one week, one month, one year, or one entire lifetime. Life is amazing and it does not lose its wonder and magic because we are given an expiration date. As a matter of fact that event may be the catalyst that helps us find the true joy and meaning in life. Think about it: Could it be that the very acceptance of the inevitability of our own death can lead us to live life more fully? I will spend a great deal of this book proving just that, because in accepting our own mortality with no sense of fear, we are ultimately freed to embrace life.

I may challenge you throughout this book to push yourself farther than you want to go and what I can promise you in return is that if you would open your heart and mind to the possibilities in these pages, you could discover that death is the reward for living fully and from a place of love. You may see that when we live all in, our final days can be a mirror of that life and we could die exactly as we lived. At this point you may be wondering: How will I face my own death? The answer to that question lies within each of us. It is my hope that this book will help you accept your dying process as the culmination of a magnificent life. If you can do this, you may truly find "joy in dying."

ONE

"I consciously filled my heart with love—love of life, love of death, love of anger, love of hate, love of longing, love of regret, love of disappointment, just *Love*. And then I entered my brother's reality."

1

Neil's Story

Let's begin with the entirety of how I ended up helping my older brother Neil through his dying process. I had not spoken to my brother in over twenty years except for two brief times that he was in the hospital. He had been involved with drugs and alcohol for most of his life, and out of loyalty to people in my family who had been hurt by him I had cut all ties. I am sad to say that my own two children never even met my brother. So how did it come about that I was the one who was there in his time of need? How is it that I got the blessing of helping him transition from this world? I cannot answer the latter question but I can explain how I came to be by his side.

It was a typical morning in Las Vegas, where I had gone to secure the home of my son, who had recently been deployed to Afghanistan. In Las Vegas, I had found the time and space to pursue my master's degree in counseling, and so I had stayed on. Las Vegas had also offered me the opportunity to expand my knowledge of the many different techniques available to help me identify what I call "My Truth," and I was learning how to connect to that "knowing" that existed within me. I attended countless workshops and retreats to further enhance this ability to listen to what lay deep within me; and to hear the voice that exists in each of us that tells us what to do, when to do it, and how to do it. As part of my daily practice, I would center myself through meditation so that I could be as in touch with my own life force as possible.

On this morning, I had just finished my meditation and was settling in to enjoy my first cup of coffee. As I sat quietly and enjoyed the warm morning, a strange sensation came over me. I had this urge inside of me, this voice telling me I needed to return to Wyoming, where I was born and where my mother and most of my siblings still lived. I was the youngest of eleven children born to a family in Casper that had a great many devout Christian members. Since my childhood, my own personal expression of faith had widened and deepened, so that I now spent time each day listening for the still small voice within me. Now that voice was urging me home, with no explanation as to why. This was such a crazy notion that I dismissed it immediately.

I had just returned from Wyoming two weeks earlier and was on schedule to attend a retreat in about two weeks, a retreat might I add, that I had already paid for. But the feeling continued to grow inside of me. I argued with myself that, no, it was definitely not a good time to return to Wyoming. I continued enjoying my coffee but the voice in me just kept getting stronger and stronger. It was now telling me that not only must I go back but that I also needed to prepare to stay for an extended period of time. I had had these callings before but never as strong as this one. The feeling just wouldn't go away. I began to make calls, checking on my friends and family to make sure everyone was okay and that it was not energy surrounding them that was calling me to Wyoming. To my relief everyone was fine; I could let go of any notion of returning.

I began to get ready for the day but the feeling just would not subside. Instead the voice kept getting louder. I tried every argument to quiet it but it persisted. I was literally talking to myself, saying, "No, I just got back to Vegas and I have this retreat in a couple of weeks. I cannot go." I turned to my class work so I could drown out the voice. But nothing would make it go away and finally, with much reluctance, I loaded up the car and headed back to Wyoming. Two hours into the trip I received the phone call that would start me on a journey that would teach me profound lessons about life and death.

It was my sister, the one who had been hurt the worst by my brother Neil. She said our brother was ill and that his daughter, who lived some fifty miles away, had called to let her know that he was being transported to hospice that day. She said the hospital had told her that the doctor had given Neil forty-eight hours to live. My sister was distraught because she was the only one available to help with the process of getting him settled at the hospice; all our other siblings worked full time, and as the only one of us who worked from home, she had often borne the brunt of family caregiving. I told her not to worry, that I was already on my way; she would not have to handle this one. I knew helping Neil would push her to the limit; there was so much that was still unresolved between them. I arrived in Casper the next day.

As I entered Neil's room at hospice, I experienced a rush of familiar memories—memories from seven years before when our father died of lung cancer. There really is a smell to cancer, and I was inundated with that unforgettable odor the minute I entered my brother's room. The twenty years since we had last spoken had been much harder on him than it had been on me. Neil looked so *worn* for lack of a better word. His body seemed shriveled and his face was wrinkled with the wear of aging, drinking, partying, and oh yes, the cancer. As I began to examine this man, the very thought of whom for so many years had filled me with contempt and anger, a new feeling came over me. I knew at once that my last few years of attending spiritual retreats and honing my spiritual practice, which was based on love, were going to be put to the ultimate test. How would I go from that place of not being willing to be in the same room as this man to now being the person who would help him transition out of his body. I knew this was my calling; everything in my soul was speaking to me. This was the duty to which I was charged. I was here to help this man who had been the source, or so I thought at the time, of so much pain in my family. I was feeling insecure and wondering why this extraordinary challenge had been placed on my shoulders.

I was alone with this bitter, hateful man. He was mean to everyone who entered the room. Where would I begin? I went to the nurses' station to see if they had any information or advice for me. What had worked with other difficult patients?

How did they deal with this sort of behavior on a daily basis? What was my brother going through? What was his prognosis?

The nurses told me a story of ranting, raving, and my brother fighting them on every move they made. "He is a tough one," they said. "Death is going to be difficult." I explained that I was experienced in the dying process as just a few years back my father had passed. I soon realized that this was a much different situation; my father, even though he fought hard to keep death away, was an extremely loving man.

The nurses shared that my brother had said he was ready to die but was very afraid of what lay ahead for him, and that fear consumed him. His greatest fear appeared to be the fear of hell. Throughout the twenty-four hours since he had arrived, he had talked of little else except when he was screaming and cursing the nurses out. I took a moment to center myself. I had traveled 975 miles for this. I reminded myself that my belief that love is all we need was going to be put to the ultimate test. "Okay, here goes," I whispered to myself, and I consciously filled my heart with love—love of life, love of death, love of anger, love of hate, love of longing, love of regret, love of disappointment, just *Love*. And then I entered my brother's reality.

Neil was quite agitated because they had told him for the umpteenth time that he was not allowed to smoke in the room and that he would have to go outside if he wished to have a cigarette. The effort to get him into the wheelchair and hooked up to the portable oxygen system was extreme, but finally our mission was accomplished. The hospice house had a beautiful garden area and so we proceeded to make our way outside. This place became our haven. It was where we formed the bond of two people just loving one another and accepting each other in spite of our flaws and insecurities and a long history of negative emotion.

Our conversation began simply enough. I felt we needed to spend just a small amount of time cleaning up the past, not to delve too deeply, just enough to clear the air. I began: "Neil I am sorry for the last twenty years in which I shut off communication with you." I expected self-pity and condemnation but what came from him next was very different. "No, I wasn't available," he said. "The drugs and alcohol were all I wanted, and I was surrounded by people who participated in those things."

I said I understood, but that was no excuse for me turning my back on him. He said he was sorry too. Then the first miracle unfolded. We looked each other in the eyes and I said, "I guess that's all that needs to be said. You have such a small amount of time left on this earth. We should spend it in the here and now." He agreed. But a moment later he began his ranting. He ranted about the neighbors, his friends who turned on him, the anger that he was ill and in this place, the hatred he had for the nurses, the food, and anything else associated with the hospice. He said they were going to kill him. I stared at him and stated the obvious: "No, it is the cancer that is killing you, not the medicine the nurses are dispensing." He continued his ranting and I allowed him some time with that. I thought: After all, he is dying; maybe he can be allotted time to express some anger.

Presently Neil began to grow calmer and that is when I began. I explained that anger is usually just a mask for fear, and I asked him to name his biggest fear in this moment, right here and now. His response was that the medicine they were giving him was going to kill him. I again stated the obvious: "No, but the cancer is."

"Jesus Christ! Don't you think I know that?" he barked at me. I said no I wasn't sure he understood that. For a moment our eyes met again and he could see there was no sarcasm in my eyes, just love and understanding. I asked my question again. What do you fear the most? "I am afraid everyone is going to steal my stuff," he said. I observed that in the grand scheme of things what did it matter? He was dying and wouldn't need it. It took a couple hours of much similar conversation for him to arrive at the notion that it really didn't matter. All that mattered was right here and now.

The "here and now" had never been a place where my brother had lived. He lived in the past, where there was regret and anger at his having spent so many years as an alcoholic. I again asked Neil to just share with me his biggest fear. He said it was that he wasn't forgiven for his sins. Awesome! Now we had something to work with!

Neil told me that he had begged God for forgiveness and didn't feel like he had it yet. I said, "Oh yes, you have been forgiven by God. That happened the moment you asked." I suggested that the issue lay in the fact that even though God had forgiven him, he hadn't forgiven himself and the other people who he felt had harmed him in some way. I told him again how sorry I was for our lack of communication over the past twenty years. He said at once, "Oh, don't be sorry." But I persisted. "I am sorry," I told him, and then I asked, "Will you please forgive me?"

'Okay, I will but you didn't do anything wrong," he said.

I responded: "Yes, Neil. I did. I am acknowledging my share of the responsibility for us not communicating. I also want you to know I forgive you for your part and for all the things that I held against you."

The look he gave me told the story as tears welled in his eyes.

"You forgive me?" he said softly.

"Absolutely, and Neil I haven't said this for a long time but I love you."

The feeling in the air that autumn night can never be duplicated. It was a moment in which two people really forgave one another and the bond of unconditional love was forged.

We spent the next few hours talking about death and how he envisioned the process. I knew his view was far different from mine. I asked him if he believed he was going to heaven and to my surprise he responded, "Yes." Oh, what a gift! This would make the process much smoother. He said he was very scared still and would I stay with him until the end. I said, "Yes of course, I will hold your hand as you leave this earth."

It was now time to begin the next step. I knew Neil had to find a way to forgive himself in order to address his fear, regret, pain and self-pity. We had come far in a mere six hours; it was crazy how fast Neil was progressing. He had gone from screaming and yelling to a small semblance of acceptance. He reflected that he did not fear death so much as he feared how he was going to pass. The most amazing hospice nurse I have ever encountered came outside right then. She explained what would happen to him physically and that they would make him as comfortable as possible. And when the breathing got worse, they would administer more drugs to diminish his suffering. She spent an hour just talking with us, gently helping Neil understand the physical aspects of the dying process. This was another turning point because with that fear relieved, we could get to the heart of the matter—his forgiveness of himself for the life he had led.

I began exploring Neil's feelings about his life. What had he done "right," what had he done "wrong?" Once we identified the areas of regret, it was such a simple matter. We spent a few more hours talking and dealing with the issue of self-forgiveness. Oh, how we punish ourselves by withholding this forgiveness. Never would we punish another as harshly as we do ourselves. In general, the forgiveness of another comes with far less effort. But we will spend years punishing ourselves. I told him he had spent enough of his sixty-seven years punishing himself, and that whatever he had done did not deserve a death sentence. He had punished his body with drugs and alcohol and self-abuse and it was time to release all that. It was time to just accept what had been and move forward. Life sentences are normally reserved for killers, and he was not a killer, so it was time to let go so he could fully experience peace in the last few days he had. Again the speed at which this all took place astounds me even to this day. It is a testament to the incredible power of love. Right there on that back porch he forgave himself and cried for what was left undone and for a life he felt he had not fully lived.

I stayed with him at the hospice, only leaving for a few hours each day to shower and refresh. Early on the third day, I invited my family to meet their brother and son. The man they encountered in that room was a Neil who had not lived on this earth before, a man he always wanted to be. My family came in one by one, impressed with the peace that was exhibited by my brother. There were times of struggle throughout the day but we welcomed each family member and I protected him from those who could not accept the idea that he was living a new life, forbidding some from returning to see him. He had worked hard in the last twenty-four hours and he deserved to live this new life free of rancor, to just revel in the moment. He lived so completely in those last days, sharing joy and peace with all who were interested.

Lastly came the time with his three children, who were now in their late twenties and early thirties. His children came even though the relationships with each had been almost nonexistent. It was a miracle to watch the relationships grow and flourish in those last days. He embraced his children with love and gratitude for their lives, and they embraced him in return.

The hospice staff originally told me that Neil had maybe two to four days to live, but he lived a total of ten days—ten glorious days in which this man was able to be in the moment and transform into his higher self. I have often said it does not matter if you reach the point of full self-expression for one hour, one day or one month; it is the reaching it that is important, the beauty is in making it to this higher vibrational level regardless of the duration. I can rest in the complete knowledge that Neil lived completely in this lifetime. I am awe every time I tell the story. It is amazing how much life he was able to experience in ten short days. He said that he felt the greatest joy, peace and love he had ever known in those last days of his life, then he thanked me and asked how he could repay me. I said it was not necessary. The gift he had already given me was more than enough. I will never forget this time with my brother as long as I live on this earth.

TWO

"When a loved one is dying the family often comes together around that person. We celebrate and feel joy in our ability to touch, kiss, caress, laugh and cry with the dying person. I would add that just as there is generally joy in the birthing process, with the right perspective, there can be immense joy in the dying process, too."

2

Joy in Dying

It is critical before we delve more deeply into the idea of finding joy in dying that we do a quick overview of the steps involved. First, I want to explore how the birthing process is similar to the dying process. I will then explain the importance of acceptance and introduce the concept of unconditional love. I will begin a discussion on the role of forgiveness in the dying process, and I will explore the idea of living in the here and now as it pertains to dying. I will also briefly touch on how the dying person's perspective on life after death affects the process and I will talk a little about cherishing each moment. Much of this discussion will tend to be clinical but please bear with me, as it is fundamental in setting the stage for the chapters to come.

Let's start with what many people may consider to be completely absurd. I must confess that many years ago I, too, would have rolled my eyes at the mention of such idiocy—the peculiar viewpoint that the dying process is like the birthing process. This may seem to many to be a crazy notion at first, but let's look more closely at how they compare.

There are few certainties in life but two things are inevitable for all members of the human race, and no, I'm not talking about death and taxes, but rather birth and dying. We all must experience the birthing process to become present on this earth and we all must experience the dying process to leave this earth. Most of us want to believe death happens to someone else, someone else's child, parent, spouse, brother, sister, anyone other than us and ours. The reality however, is the moment we gasp for our first breath we are simultaneously taking the first step towards death. Now I know that sounds a bit morbid but it is truly not meant to offend. There was a time I would have taken offense as well, but I now accept the fact that I will die as simply a part of life. I have made peace with the inevitability of death, thus creating a space for me to live each day of my life as if I am dying because I know that I am.

The prelude to death is often pain and sickness and so is the prelude to birth. During the dying process we may experience sickness due to medical treatment or a terminal disease itself may cause symptoms. We may experience swelling, weight gain or weight loss and bouts of nausea. We may develop additional ailments such as anemia, diabetes, and organ malfunction. We may have periods of extreme pain.

Now let's examine how that compares to pregnancy. During pregnancy we experience morning sickness, swelling of the body in general, and weight gain. Many people develop anemia, diabetes, and yes in rare instances organ malfunction. There is pain in the development stage as our body makes room for the growing child within us, and extreme pain as the child exits our body through the birthing process. As one may see, the prelude to birth and the prelude to death can have similar effects on the body.

Pregnancy and the dying process are similar in other ways as well, depending on what you believe happens to us when we die. Many faiths see death with all its attendant pain and uncertainty, as the passage to a bright and beautiful afterlife, just as birth, also painful and uncertain, is a passage to a potentially joyous new life on earth. If you don't believe in life after death, you might take comfort in the tranquility of nothingness, of energy transmuted into all things, and most especially, the life that a loved one who has passed away continues to have in our memories. In this way, both birth and death are passages to a new way of being on this earth.

Now, I realize many of you may take issue with these ideas, but please stay with me for a little longer as I make the last and maybe most relevant comparison. The effects of dying and birthing on the family are really very similar. When there is a diagnosis of death for a family member, the entire family must begin to envision a new normal that does not include the dying person. The family dynamic is forever changed by the impending absence of this member just as when pregnancy occurs the family dynamic changes in preparation for the addition of another person. Death literally occurs in both instances: The pair having the child faces the death of the couple and begins the challenge of developing a family of three souls together. The relationship goes through many changes as the couple prepares for the entry of a new being. In a similar way, death creates a new dynamic for the family that must face the exit of a loved one. The family members need to learn to function without this intricate piece to their puzzle, without the presence of mother, father, brother, sister, son, or daughter. It changes everything about the family and how they interact regardless of what place the person holds.

Pregnancy gives birth to a new life, adding joy to the family with the baby's soft skin, infant smiles, cuddling and laughter. The baby brings the family together to celebrate and welcome the new life into being. Although the experiences are for a shorter duration, dying can mirror this joy. When a loved one is dying the family often comes together around that person. We celebrate and cherish in our ability to touch, kiss, caress, laugh and cry with the dying person. We feel gratitude that we are able to express love and create new memories with that person that will live on as long as we ourselves are breathing on this earth. I would take this analogy even further: I would add that just as there is generally joy in the birthing process, with the right perspective, there can be immense joy in the dying process too.

So how do we attain a joyful perspective on dying? I will briefly outline here the ideas that will be covered in subsequent chapters as we explore more deeply the answer to this question. Though these ideas can be approached in any order, acceptance is the first step we will address simply because it opens the space for the other steps to develop. Acceptance is twofold: We have to accept our mortality and we also have to accept our way of being in the world and how we have created our relationships with others. This is fundamental to transforming our relationships in positive ways during our dying process.

A related concept in finding the joy in dying is learning to love unconditionally. This is the love that has no conditions or restraints upon it, and it is not contingent upon reciprocation. Unconditional love is *being* love, not feeling love. This may be difficult to grasp at first, but unconditional love has nothing to do with feeling anything. Instead, it is being the true essence of love regardless of what is going on outside or inside of the physical body. Unconditional love is being present in the moment to the point that there is nothing *but* love. This love is not the romantic love that most of us fall into; it is not the love of a parent for a beloved child; it is a state of *being* love. This way of looking at love is completely different than the ways in which we are used to expressing love and it may take time to embrace it fully, but it is important to begin exploring the idea of "being" love rather than being "in" love or "feeling" love.

Another step in the dying process is to identify what your views of death are. What, if anything, do you think happens when we die? This is important for the one dying or for the caregiver of the one dying. Many of you have an idea of what you believe will happen after death but I am talking about getting a clear vision in your mind of what the afterlife looks like *for you*. This will be imperative, especially at the end, and it may make the difference between struggling for your last breath and simply letting go with peace. Be sure you are clear in this vision and if you are the one dying, take the time to communicate your views to your family or the people responsible for your care. It will help them help you if they know the goal you are trying to achieve.

Although this step is important in the process and can't be skipped, this book does not go into detail about what happens after death. People have many different visions of life after death but the purpose of getting clear about your own beliefs is not really about death. It is about living life to the fullest whether you have one week, one month, one year, or twenty years. The sole purpose of this book is to help you find joy in the dying process, which has absolutely nothing to do with death and everything to do with life.

This brings us to another important step on this journey called dying, which is to become present in the here and now. Oh, how easy it seems, for after all isn't that exactly where we are? We are right here dealing with living—and yet at the same time we are being asked to deal with the consequences of the past and the reality of dying at some point in the future. It is a game of cat and mouse, finding a way to live in the here and now, yet come to terms with our past while making a way for the future, all at the same time. We must fully embrace everything just as it is, and just as it was, and just as will or will not be. This step in the dying process is difficult at best because we so want things to be different. We don't want the prognosis of death and yet that is our reality as humans. We want to change the past and yet there is no way to go back. We want to have a future to look forward to but again the future may be quite limited. We will further explore this concept of the here and now in later chapters but for now I would like everyone to try to wrap their mind around the idea that living in the present moment offers the best chance of having an amazing future regardless of duration of that future.

This leads us to perhaps the most crucial step in the process of dying with joy—forgiveness. This is the step that will help us to accept our mortality without fear, to love unconditionally, and to fully embrace the here and now. Forgiveness is the key to living clearly in the present moment, for it is through forgiveness that we can put the past in the past where it belongs and transform our relationships. If we try to move forward without forgiveness, change is impossible. We must forgive those who we feel have hurt, offended, or damaged us or we cannot fully embrace that person and create the relationship for which we long. Forgiveness is the soul's way of letting go of any energy binding us to the past relationship and through that act we release ourselves from any pain caused by our connection to that human being. Even if we want to terminate the relationship, unless we forgive, true release of that person cannot occur. It may seem absurd to you that forgiveness is so significant and necessary in the dying process, but once we explore what it means to truly forgive others—and yourself— you will have a greater understanding of the tremendous power of that act.

The upcoming chapters of this book will help you to further explore finding joy in the dying through the steps outlined here. There is no definitive order to the steps that allow us to be at peace in the dying process, but for the sake of helping you discover how to find the joy in dying I must choose an order to discuss each idea. But what I want you to understand is that each of these steps becomes a comingling of ideas and consciously chosen acts. When you embark on this process, you will likely find yourself weaving from one idea into another and then back to the first. This dance continues throughout our lives as we discover new ways to work the steps and add to our repertoire.

Each concept will be discussed in detail to assist you in embracing the steps, either for yourself, or for one who is dying. Each and every one of us will at some time or another face dying. My dream is that this book will somehow help that process be filled with love, peace, and most of all joy. Every one of us can learn to live fully in the moments we have left on this great planet called earth. My goal is to enable the dying person to leave a legacy of hope by constructing a path to peace and understanding for the family that is left behind. Together, we can build a foundation for that family to continue healing long after the loved one has passed.

THREE

"Regardless of all the other Truths about life and death, can we all agree on love and peace? Can it be that acceptance is the key to unlocking this loving, peaceful, joyful state of being?."

3

Acceptance

I have decided to begin the dance with a discussion of acceptance, again not because it is necessarily the first step but because it can help ease you into the other steps. Acceptance is a fundamental part of the dying process. It is a two-step process: First, we must accept our own mortality and then we must accept ourselves, and others, just as we are and just as we are not. Both require that we suspend judgment and refrain from adding any meaning. Everything is what it is and what it is not. We simply accept that it "is."

If you will recall in Neil's story one of the first things we established was the understanding that he in fact was dying, that it was not the hospice nurses and the drugs they were giving him that would kill him; it was the cancer. For those of you who are reading this book who have been diagnosed with a terminal illness, accept that you are dying and that your death may be coming sooner than you originally anticipated. And those of you who have not been given an expiration date, you too must accept that you are dying. We are all dying. The process began the minute we took our first breath. So accept it. No one gets out of here alive!

Accepting our own mortality can make even the most courageous of people weak in the knees. No one wants to think of his or her own demise. We spend millions in drugs and alcohol and frenetic activity fending off the mere thought of it. Death happens to other people, not me. It is as if we are saying to ourselves *I am going to live forever,* which in a sense is true, because forever for you is when you take your last breath, which of course occurs at the same moment in which you die. I don't mean to trivialize this occurrence, as I understand as well as anyone the fear of dying.

If you recall, the idea of death used to send shivers through me. But while I do not want to experience death in the near future, my own or anyone else's, no longer do I fear it. I know that at some point in the future I will die. I also know that I am ready for whatever life has to offer me. I have accepted that I am not immortal and I live my life accordingly. I live most days in peace and harmony. I try my best to make the world a better place by making my corner of it as loving as it can be. I accept my death, I forgive those around me, I forgive myself, I try my best not to judge others, I love unconditionally, and I live in the here and now. Now am I perfect at these tasks? Absolutely not, but for the most part I embrace them all, which means that I live as if I am dying.

Remember earlier I hinted that I may push you farther than you might ever want to be pushed? Well, it begins now. I know for many this thought of death can cause complete anxiety but truly it cannot be avoided. It is our human reality. Eventually we are all going to die. Now sit with that for a moment. Try to wrap your mind around that idea. Just let the thought settle in. Feel yourself releasing any judgment about the fact; just embrace that it is true—you will eventually die. As you sit in the quiet with this idea, feel your body begin to relax, feel the unease lifting from your mind, let the idea rest. Just accept that it is going to happen. Notice that once you accept this as reality the anxiety associated with it begins to lighten. Spend some quiet time each day just sitting with this idea that you are dying; continue this daily meditation until you have, for the most part, eliminated any anxiety related to the fact that you are dying.

Now let's address the second step of acceptance, which is accepting ourselves exactly as we are, and others exactly as they are, without judgment. For the most part we accept our own ideas so I will focus more on accepting other peoples' ideas about themselves and their lives. What do I mean by this sort of acceptance? I am talking about genuinely accepting other people's points of view. Listening to them without argument and truly hearing their perspective on, for example, what happens after we die, without needing to change it or add to it. Listening to how they feel about life, love, happiness, and what brings them joy. Just listening to another person's point of view without judgment—this is acceptance.

In my own life, I listen to what people say is important to them. I listen to how they are feeling about all the aspects of their lives. How are their relationships with other people? Do they want to further develop those relationships? I just listen, without judgment, to how they view the world. For a moment sit back and, without inflicting your own views, let the other person tell you what is important to them in life. This is an integral part of my everyday life. It is imperative that you as the person taking care of a dying person listen to what he or she believes, helping him or her to feel heard—without judgment.

Not judging others can be extremely difficult for humans because many have an ingrained idea of what life and death look like, and are relatively sure theirs is the right view. They just know that if they say the right thing they can convince everyone that they have all the right answers. But what if there are no right answers? What if that belief is only right for them, and each person has to find what is right for him or her? Can it even be conceived that all people have the right answer for themselves? Is there a way to allow their belief to just be without imposing another opinion?

Now consider the fact that everyone has the right pieces to their own puzzle; that right here inside they know the Truth of themselves. Not that they know the Truth of others but they know their own Truth. Doesn't it hold true that if we know our own Truth then everyone else out there knows his or her own Truth, too? That inside each and every one of us is this fundamental Truth that is right for us and us alone? There doesn't have to be one Truth for everyone, because each person knows what is right for him or her.

Seriously consider how you feel about what you believe about life and death. Don't you know that no matter what anyone says, you hold your own Truth? I am convinced that most people have answered: *Yes, I know the Truth of me.* Some of your Truths say that there is a heaven and hell; some of your Truths say there is nothing after we die; some of your Truths say there is a God and some say there is not. Some say there is a Higher Universal Mind and some say not. Some of you believe in life after death and some of you do not. There are so many Truths.

Now further consider, what if each us holds the Truth for ourselves and we don't need to spend the last days of our lives arguing our Truth. If that were true, then we could spend the rest of our lives loving, honoring, enjoying, rejoicing, and living in peace and harmony. In studying different belief systems, from Christian to Buddhist to Atheist to Hindu to Muslim to Agnostic, it appears that there are two general commonalities: A desire for a life filled with love and a desire to live a life filled with peace. Most want to love another and most want to find a way to make this world more peaceful.

So if the idea is entertained that no matter what we each believe, *we all want love and peace,* isn't that the common ground we seek? Yet in the fight to convince others to think differently, we may be creating exactly the opposite of love and peace? When faced with the end, either our own or a loved one's, we may try to convince people that we have the answers to what's going to happen, when in fact all we need to do in the last days of our lives is concentrate on loving one another and finding peace? Just accept one another, and love and peace follow. Can it be that simple? It is, isn't it? Regardless of all the other Truths about life and death, can we agree on love and peace? Can it be that acceptance is the key to unlocking this loving, peaceful, joyful state of being?

I am not talking about adopting the other person's way of life, just simply allowing both opinions to exist and instead of arguing about whose views is right, concentrate all effort towards accepting people as they are and creating love and peace. Every day upon awakening the goal is to create love and peace in the world. What can be accomplished then? Could we lend a hand to a stranger, hold the door for someone, sit beside a dying person and let him be who they are? Can it be said that it matters not what he/she believes, instead that the important thing is to create a space of complete love and peace, and everything else will follow?

If it is found to be true that whether you are Christian, Buddhist, Hindu, or Atheist, we all want relationships that are loving and we all want to leave a mark in this world, does anything else matter? Could it be all we want to say is "Hey I was here?" Look at what I left as my legacy. I made a mark on my family, my friends, my co-workers, and my world. I left this place better than I found it and in the end that is a life worth living."

Now to address those who feel as if they haven't left that mark? Guess what? It is not too late. It's never too late if we still have breath. It does not matter if you live your higher self for one minute, one hour, one month, or one year. All that matters is that you live it. So right here and right now just "be" love and peace. Resolve in this very moment that anything that is not love and peace will no longer be allowed in your thoughts or your life. Let go of your judgments that your view is the right one and instead replace it with a commitment to love and peace. When we live in peace and love, people will know that we are living our Truth, and there will be no need for arguments. Be vigilant and conscious of your thoughts and choose only those that foster an acceptance of others and their points of view. Any feeling you have that is not born of peace and love, replace it. Anyone can do it. I know, I have; you can too? Now am I perfect in every moment? Absolutely not, but I am in a place of love, peace, and acceptance a good percentage of the time.

Please allow for the luxury of experiencing peace and love even for the briefest of moments. I went into my brother's room in hospice and found a man filled with anger and regret and within thirty-six short hours, he had found love and peace. He had gone from a ranting, raging alcoholic to a man who was saying please and thank you to his nursing staff and to me. Anyone can do it too. Just decide today, accept others exactly as they are. Remembering that one can hold their Truth while others can hold their Truth; neither negates the other. When each day is approached with this spirit of acceptance, then life can be lived in a place of pure peace and love. Can you imagine if that is the mark left behind?

FOUR

"If you knew this was your last moment on this earth, could you honestly allow yourself to die without offering forgiveness? Or could you say, "I forgive myself and others for being human"? Could you in that last moment "give" yourself love? Because every time you speak the words, "I forgive" you can replace those words with, "For I give.""

4

Forgiveness

The dance continues. We have explored the acceptance part of the dying process and I hope that it has brought some peace to your life, knowing you don't have to prove your beliefs nor argue anyone else's point of view. You can just accept that there are differences and that is okay. I hope, too, that you have begun to feel some sense of peace and love in your life. This next step should enhance that feeling.

Forgiveness such a simple word, but not always a simple task. How many times have we spoken the words, "I forgive you?" I myself have said them again and again in my lifetime. When I look back now, however, I realize how casually they were spoken. I might have thought I had forgiven the person but I still held resentment in my heart. They were just words I spoke without a true measure of their meaning, and for many of you reading this, the same is probably true. What I now know is that forgiveness is much more difficult than I originally thought. While I was one of those people who willingly said,

"Of course I forgive you"—and trust me, I really did want to forgive—the problem was, I didn't know *how* to forgive.

When true forgiveness occurs, your body is filled with serenity. You literally release all the meaning that you attached to the act that caused you pain and hurt. In your heart you feel calmness and gratitude. You are grateful that you let go and you feel free because you have released the hold the person who hurt you had on you. When was the last time you forgave someone and felt at peace? Have you ever felt that sense of relief? If your answer is yes, congratulations, you know just what I mean. But if your answer is no, read on and I will try to explain the "act of forgiveness."

The thing to understand is that forgiveness is much more complex than just saying the words I forgive you. Forgiveness is a feeling. And it is an action. The first step is to get clear on what you feel the offending party did to you and to try to discover the impact it has had on your life. What resentment towards that person are you harboring? How long has it been going on? What would it take for you to truly let go of the resentment you hold against the offender? Are you *willing* to let go? With all that I am I hope your answer is yes because you cannot be truly free until you do. I have said it a thousand times and I will say it a thousand times more, forgiveness is a gift we give ourselves. That's because the resentment you feel toward the person who hurt you lives inside you. It is poisoning *you*, not the other person. Even though it may seem that a willingness to forgive lets the other person off too easy, in fact, when we hold on to anger, betrayal and hurt, we're the ones who suffer in the long run. Negative feelings can show up as arthritis, diabetes, cancer and other ailments, or they can trigger mental health problems such as depression, addictions to alcohol, sex, drugs, and unhealthy relationships. When we refuse to forgive others we are effectively giving them the keys to our happiness and freedom. But when we become willing to forgive, we begin to release the anger and the pain in our hearts and in our bodies. By practicing forgiveness we are able to let go of these negative emotions and regain control of our lives. By truly forgiving another you create space for joy and peace to enter your heart. This is why I say forgiveness is a gift you give yourself.

This process will give you a clear picture of exactly what impact your hurt has had on your life, and what you stand to gain in peace and love and freedom through forgiveness. As you examine all the details, you can discover exactly how strong a hold the resentment you are harboring has on you. The deeper it reaches into your everyday life, the harder it will be to process but remember you have the strength inside you to forgive and let go. If someone spoke badly about you, the resentment may be mild and it will be fairly simple to work through the process. If however you are dealing with a more radical offense, for instance a spouse who betrayed you by having an affair or a parent who abandoned you, this process will be more intense and far reaching. But regardless of what has happened, no matter how great the pain, you must clear up the past.

So how do you do that? Start by acknowledging that you are holding on to hurt and resentment, and that you are harboring in you some ill feelings towards the other person. I know this may be difficult to admit because we all want to believe that we are "good" people and we would never wish ill against someone. But if you are not feeling at peace about a situation, you are holding on to resentment, so just own it. There is nothing wrong with this feeling. It is natural that when someone causes you pain or distress you will be angry, hurt, afraid or resentful. Without judgment, observe these feelings. Know that it is okay to feel them. It is part of being human, so accept them. Just settle into the feelings without letting them overtake you.

Once you acknowledge that the feelings exist, stop and examine where and how they are having a negative impact on your life. Does your fear of getting hurt keep you from letting people in? Is your anger keeping you from forming positive relationships? Are you afraid to let people mean something to you? Are you withholding love from others and yourself because you harbor such resentment in your life? Are you afraid that history will repeat itself? If you are honest with yourself, you will very likely answer yes to one or more of these questions.

Now what is the ultimate cost to you? When we hold onto resentment, we close off our heart to some extent. This is not to say you do not love people. You can love people with a partial heart but what I can tell you from experience is once you let go of that resentment you will be able to love others completely and more importantly you will be able to love yourself. Regardless of how minor the resentment is that you are harboring, it has closed off a part of your heart. It has made your life smaller.

So how do we forgive? Well first we have to understand what forgiveness is not. Forgiveness is not condoning the act of the other person. It is not saying what they did was okay. It is not saying that we weren't hurt by the act. And it by no means says we have to continue a relationship with the offender. Quite the contrary, forgiving the other person allows us to completely break any hold they might have had on us. We may at last be able to turn away from the offender for good, but with peace and harmony in our hearts instead of feelings of hurt and bitterness and pain.

Viewed another way, forgiveness is the act of not allowing the offending party to have an impact on our life in the future. It clears the path for us to move forward, unhampered by whatever happened in the past. Forgiveness in this sense is letting go of any meaning we attached to the act that hurt us. If someone betrayed us, let it simply be that. Say: "This person betrayed me but I am no longer allowing this person to have a negative impact on my life. I am no longer letting that mean something about my worth as a person. I release any and all feelings of worthlessness I might have harbored as a result of the act that hurt me. I no longer choose to allow the offender to have any control in my life." Again, understand you are not saying that what they did is okay. You are instead saying that even though they hurt you, they will no longer have any power at all over you.

Forgiveness is seldom easy. In fact it may well prove to be one of the most difficult tasks we will ever undertake in our lives. That act of letting go requires courage, integrity and compassion for oneself. Releasing the anger, the pain, and the fear is not for the faint of heart. It is difficult to forgive the parent who seemed not to care, the man that molested you at the tender age of seven, the friend who wasn't there for you in your time of need, or the husband who cheated on your marriage. These people may have caused you pain, but holding on to the resentment is extending their chokehold on your life. You are not able to fully love another, you are not able to fully love yourself, and in many areas you probably feel stuck. And what did the original betrayal say about you anyway? Nothing. That's the fact.

Now the story that you may have told yourself is that these people were against you in some way, that they treated you the way they did because you weren't good enough, or because they wanted to hurt you. The truth is that you were hurt by their actions, but aren't you now perpetuating that pain by holding on to the resentment? *Yes, you are.* You can go on denying this fact but what I can tell you is that if you do not forgive and release the hold they have on you, it will manifest into sickness, sadness, or depression somewhere in your life. You may go on living and you may even be able to convince yourself that all is well but sooner or later, the resentment will fester and affect your life.

By forgiving you eliminate any possibility of this continuing to hurt you. You start by saying: "I release any hold this act has on my life. I forgive the person who committed this act and by doing so I release myself to live a full life; a life filled with love and compassion. I do not condone what this person did, and this forgiveness does not mean I will necessarily have any further contact with this person. This forgiveness does not say what they did was okay, and it does not say that I was not hurt. What it does say is that regardless of how this person's actions made me feel, I am now releasing all control it has in my life. I am releasing all feelings of resentment that I feel towards this person and I am releasing myself from the burden of having to hold on to those feelings of resentment. This person's actions will no longer have any effect on me."

We have talked about releasing the resentment and forgiving the offender, now it is time to take the last and most difficult step in the forgiveness process. This is the step that most counselors and books on forgiveness forget to address. The last and final person you need to forgive is yourself. Every time we hold resentment or feel hurt, it places us in a situation where we need to forgive ourselves. And sometimes we, too, have to forgive ourselves for hurtful actions we have taken against another person. This can be the hardest step—forgiving ourselves for allowing someone else to have control or for feeling the way we did or acting the way we did. Every instance is an opportunity for us to say, "I'm sorry for allowing the pain I felt to have a negative impact on my life." "I am sorry for holding on to resentments that kept me from loving others and myself to my full ability." "I forgive myself for allowing my resentments to create illness in my life." "I forgive myself for allowing anyone else's acts to create discontent and anxiety in my life." "I forgive myself for the ways in which I have hurt another person." "I forgive myself for allowing hate and negativity to come into my life." These words when spoken out loud, can literally free your soul.

Forgiveness is releasing any hold the past has on us so we can move forward. I will boldly say that without true forgiveness, the kind that brings absolute peace to your soul, you will never be able to completely move into the future nor completely love yourself or others. Forgiveness is the gateway to a full life—and a joyful death.

I will use my brother's example as a guide. I had not spoken to my brother in over twenty years when I entered his room at hospice. He had hurt members of the family and we had long ago cut off contact. When I entered his room, I knew in order for us to have any chance of moving forward we would have to clean up the past; in this case a past of abuse, drugs, and alcohol. So I began. I started by saying I was sorry for my part in our not talking for the past twenty years and in that moment I also forgave myself. I released any guilt that I had associated with that act and just simply let it be. My brother apologized, too, and we moved forward. By forgiving each other—and ourselves—we created the space for us to take the next steps towards my brother living a fully realized life in the short time he had left. I truly believe that if we had not addressed our regrets and resentments directly, they would have been the elephant in the room that kept us from making progress. Instead, the act of forgiving each other created a space for absolute healing, a place in our hearts where love and peace could grow and flourish.

The work with my brother was intense much of the time. He held a great deal of resentment towards others as well as himself but little by little he let go and released. He started with the small things. He apologized to the nurses and the other hospice staff for cursing at them. He cleaned up things with various family members, asking for forgiveness and granting forgiveness when asked. But in the end it was the final act of forgiving himself that brought him peace. He was able to forgive himself for being an alcoholic and an absent father, son, and brother. He forgave himself for causing pain to those around him and for not living what he considered a good life. He forgave himself for being angry and hateful. And in that space of forgiveness of himself, he was able to create genuine relationships with his mother, his children, and me. We created a bond of love that helped our family accept his passing.

Because of the work he completed my brother was able to die in peace. He told me shortly before he passed that he had experienced more serenity in the last six days of his life than in his entire lifetime. He thanked me for my guidance in helping him achieve that experience of pure love. I would ask you not to wait until your last six days to discover that kind of peace. Begin forgiving today; forgive like you are dying so you can experience that kind of peace throughout the remainder of your life regardless of whether that is six days, six weeks, six months or six years. Forgive, forgive, forgive and when you are done, forgive some more.

If you knew this was your last moment on this earth, that you were taking your last breath, how hard would it be to forgive? Could you honestly allow yourself to die without offering forgiveness? Or could you say, "I forgive myself and others for being human"? Could you in that last moment "give" yourself love? Because every time you speak the words, "I forgive" you can replace those words with, "For I give."

Try it: I forgive myself for feeling hate—for I give myself and others love. I forgive myself for feeling anger—for I give myself the ability to feel joy. I forgive myself for holding onto resentments—for I give myself a life filled with peace and harmony. I forgive myself for wasting my life—for I give myself endless possibilities for the future. I forgive my mother/father for not loving me the way I needed them to—for I give myself the possibility of a new loving relationship with my mother/father. I forgive the man who molested me as a child—for I give myself the possibility of a life unaffected by the pain he caused. I forgive all who offended, hurt, or abused me in any way—for I give myself a life where others' actions do not have power over me. I forgive myself for not taking responsibility for my life—for I give myself a life where I can choose to be happy, to love, and to feel peace and joy.

I hope that you now understand and believe this statement: Forgiveness has nothing to do with the ones who hurt us. It is a loving gift we give ourselves.

FIVE

"There is no shame, no fear, and no hurt in the current moment; there is just *what is*. You are just being and everything that is happening is just happening. You are not adding emotion or meaning to the moment; you are just experiencing it for everything it is and everything it is not. There is no judgment when living in the moment."

5

Here And Now

Many of you may have been tested during the previous chapter but the forgiveness work you did is crucial for this next step in the process of finding joy in dying—living in the here and now. Without forgiveness it is nearly impossible to center ourselves in the present moment and yet it is only in the here and now that we are able to transform our lives. The past is the past and nothing can be changed. It is done. The future is somewhere out in the distance and we can effect no changes there either because it hasn't yet arrived. It is only in the here and now that we can alter our circumstances and make positive adjustments to our lives. So let's begin right here and now.

As I suggested when I initially outlined the steps for making the most of the time you have left, living in the here and now gives us the best chance of having an amazing future regardless of duration of that future. Staying focused on the present can sometimes be a little tricky in that you have to find a way to live in the moment, while clearing up the messes of the past to make way for the future. When learning to live this way, you are constantly doing the tango, a dance of give and take—resolving lingering issues from the past, being attentive in the present, and looking towards the future. Living in the here and now is critical to all people but none more so than the terminally ill. If nothing can be changed in the past and nothing can be accomplished in the future, there is only the now, and in the now we have no choice but to make peace with what was, what is, and what will be.

For one who has been diagnosed with a terminal illness, it can be scary maneuvering in the here and now. There is no road map, yet your commitment to the present moment is the key to tapping into an expansive sense of joy and peace as you live out the remainder of your life. I understand that this is a frightening journey but if you are willing to travel down this road of uncertainty, it will transform your life into a beacon of love, acceptance and joy.

So how do you start a journey for which there is no one predetermined path? You start by accepting your mortality; you accept that in this moment, right here and now, you are dying. This is true for everyone, even the infant as it draws its first breath, but if you have a terminal illness, the inevitability of death is that much more real for you. It is a difficult task to live in the here and now when the future feels finite and the past is littered with regrets. I do not mean to diminish the intensity of this challenge or lessen how incredibly difficult it can be to grasp. Each and every one of us needs to understand that we are mortal but those who have been diagnosed with a terminal illness have no choice but to come to terms with death. I am not saying that you lie down and die—not at all. Rather, I am saying that once you accept that death may occur you can begin fighting to live. You do not have the luxury of procrastination that is afforded the rest of us; you are pressed to find a quicker resolution to this question of how to live joyfully and well.

Take comfort from the fact that you are not alone on this journey, even though it might feel at times as if you are. The fact is that each minute of life moves us towards death. I struggled myself to embrace this Truth, that with every intake of breath I was that much closer to my own expiration date. I say this now without judgment or meaning or fear. It just is what it is. I know that I am dying and that knowledge has created a space for me to embrace life to its fullest, to live in the moment and cherish those around me, and to be attentive to my vast blessings. So how did I get to that place of gratitude and peace? I would love to offer up some magic to help bring about this state of grace but it can only come from within you. You must look at your life and choose to accept it as it is, not as you wish it were, but just exactly how it is showing up.

Stop for a moment and just think about how you are being in the world. Become present with yourself right here and now. Breathe deeply. Become still. Now try to realize that right here and right now you have a possibility of dying; we all have that possibility every time we take a breath. Regardless of whether you have been diagnosed with a terminal illness or whether you are just walking down the street, every single one of us could die, right here and now. Think about the times that you can remember when someone suddenly died. They had a heart attack, were killed in a car crash, or died in their sleep. It could happen to any of us. We are dying every minute we are living, but no one is clearer on that fact than those who have been diagnosed with a terminal illness. One could almost say they have an advantage because they can no longer deny the Truth that they are dying. I know this may seem morbid but once we truly embrace that we could die at any moment, we can then accept the reality of our own mortality and can begin the amazing work of living life to the fullest every minute. All it takes is being present in every moment; accepting our life as it is; appreciating those around us; and being grateful for this amazing journey that we are experiencing right now.

Why then, you may ask, do I need to examine the past if the here and the now is what's truly important? To that I would respond that visiting the past is necessary because it holds the key to why we are thinking or reacting the way we are in the present. Why do we say this, do that, cry when that happens, laugh when that happens, get mad when that happens? Why do we react to certain people the way we do? The answers to these and many more questions lie in our past. Everything that happens in our lives, whether it is good or bad, happy or sad, right or wrong creates a way of being for us. We develop the idea that we "must be" this way or that way. It is the "must be" that causes the suffering in our lives and blocks the full expression of ourselves in our relationships. That single thought of "must be" was created by our reactions to things that happened to us in the past.

Some of those ways of being are working for us in our current situation and some of them are not. In order to truly live in a place of peace and love we must identify those ways of being that are working for us so we can continue to use them, and we must also identify those that are not working for us so we can implement the necessary changes. Without examining that past, it will be more difficult to change our present behavior. We use the past to identify the areas of concern and then we move forward into the here and now to take whatever actions might be needed to create our best lives. Once we are able to transform our thoughts and create new responses, we eliminate the "must be" from our vocabulary. Rather than being constrained by our past we become open to the endless possibilities that exist for us in the present and in the future.

It is necessary to understand that examining the past is very different from living in the past. I am sure most of you are accustomed to looking at your past and even your future; many of you may spend a good deal of time living there and giving scant notice to the present. I know this was true for me. I lived so much of my life in the past or the future that it was nearly impossible to live in the here and now. Being "present" in the here and now can be a difficult task. We are all physically here but to bring our thoughts and our actions into the present takes conscious and sustained attention. Think of how many times in your day you say or think, *I used to be* or *I will be*—fill in the blank. Conversely, how often you think, *I am happy right here. My life is exactly what I want right now?* Most of us, if we are honest with ourselves, rarely express such thoughts.

When I first began this process myself, I used some simple techniques to become truly present in the moment. I would concentrate with all my senses on whatever was around me. I would notice the paintings on the wall, the sound of the fan rotating, the music playing on the radio, the hiss of the tires hitting the pavement as I drove down the road, the sound of my kids yelling or laughing, or of the voice speaking to me. I would slow down and make myself notice every detail surrounding me in that moment. Try this exercise yourself. Just be present to your current environment, letting go of any judgment of how it is or how it should be. Realize what is around you. Notice every sight and sound, every smell, every person, the quality of the light, whether it's cold or warm. What do you feel right here, right now? Are you happy? Sad? Worried? Curious? Do you feel love? Do you feel anger or fear? What is present in your life in this very moment? Not yesterday, not tomorrow, but *right now*? Just feel it, don't think it, feel it. As you become "present" in this moment you will feel a peace begin to overtake you. Can you feel how it is beginning to flood your body? Now stay there for a few moments before you read any further. Notice everything, including the way the sense of peace seeps through and around your senses, supplanting any emotion you might have been feeling.

Becoming present is essential to learning to live in the here and now. A fair question is how do I know if I have successfully "presenced" myself in the moment? It is simple: There is no shame, no fear, and no hurt in the current moment; there is just *what is*. You are just being and everything that is happening is just happening. You are not adding emotion or meaning to the moment; you are just experiencing it for everything it is and everything it is not. There is no judgment when living in the moment. If it is raining, it is just raining. If you are in pain, you are just in pain. If you are sad, you are just sad. If you are dying, you are just dying.

Now I am not saying you can't or shouldn't experience emotion about what is happening. If you are mad because it is raining be mad, just don't make it mean anything other than that you are mad because it is raining. If you angry and feel like giving up because the pain is so bad, then feel the anger and frustration but don't let it mean anything other than that the pain is bad. Just feel what you feel with no resistance or added meaning. Let it wash over you and let yourself experience it. If you are dying and feeling sad about leaving your family, let yourself experience the emotion. If you are angry because you are dying, be angry. It is completely natural to have these emotions. The issue comes when we try to judge or justify the emotions. This may seem complicated but in fact it is not. The emotions are what they are. Feel them and then let them go. But what we generally try to do as humans is justify that we have a right to have these feelings and this is how we complicate our lives. We wish we weren't having the feelings or we argue that it is not fair that we have to deal with dying. What I know from experience is that once you quit arguing about whether a situation is right or wrong, fair or not fair, the struggle ends. If you can simply say it is what it is and not try to justify or fight the situation but rather just accept it for what it is and what it is not, you will no longer be limited by your circumstances. Acceptance is the precursor to all meaningful change, and the gateway to peace. When you feel this peace stirring within your heart, you will know that you are "presenced" in the moment. You are living in the here and now.

Now the real work begins. When you are given a diagnosis of terminal illness, it sends your senses into overdrive and a feeling of urgency develops within your being. The mere fact that you have been given an expiration date brings into focus the necessity of completing the tasks you have set for yourself in this life. It may feel unfair that you are having to deal with this on top of dying but in all honesty we should all be dealing with this all along because we are all dying, most of us just haven't been given an expiration date. We all long for peaceful and loving relationship in our life, yet we put off doing the one thing that would most help us achieve our goal, and that is living in this moment— releasing the hold of the past and trusting the future to take care of itself. But those who are terminally ill can no longer prolong the inevitable. They must act now, even as the rest of us go through life thinking we have forever and suffering because we are not forced into accepting and embracing life as it is.

We are all in the same predicament. Those who think they are going to live forever and those who think death happens to someone else just haven't realized the truth that they are dying. Consider how different our choices would be if we lived every moment with the mindset that we are dying, that this moment could well be the last one we were ever going to have. Would things look different to us; would we accept life as it is; would we more readily accept people as they are; and would we cherish every moment we have left? Those who are terminally ill have come face to face with this reality, but what I am challenging each of you to do is consider that you too are dying with every breath you take. Ask yourself: Are there areas of my life that I have not accepted as they are? Are there choices I am making that alienate me from friends and family, rather than bring us closer? Am I stuck in the recriminations of the past or have I forgiven everyone I need to forgive and made peace with experiences that cannot be undone?

Now I will challenge you further to consider that this is your last moment. How would your actions change? How do you want to be remembered? What legacies will your leave for family, your friends, and the world? I know that it is inherent in our being to leave the world better than we found it, and to leave our loved ones happy, healthy and at peace. As paradoxical as it may seem, the first step to making this a reality is to change our own circumstances, and we do this by living in the here and now and not letting the regrets of the past or fear of the future rule us.

In his final days, my brother Neil provided a compelling example of the transformative power that acceptance and living in the present moment can have on your family, your friends, the people around you, and on the quality of your own life. My brother had chosen to drink and smoke excessively for most of his adult life. This was his past and he powerless to change it. He could not go back and choose not to drink and smoke; the damage was already done. He then suffered through cancer. This was his present and he came to accept it as the reality in which all his actions would now be made. He could see that he was going to die in the near future, and that all he could control was what he was going to do in the here and now with the knowledge he had. He could continue to drink and smoke and die more quickly. He could take radiation and chemo to extend his life, but live out the remainder of his days angry, hurt and afraid. Or he could decide to change his life for the better right here and now. His initial choice was to live out his days angry and hurt, but with my assistance he began the work needed to heal his past so his future could be filled with joy and peace.

As he maneuvered on the slippery slope of revisiting his past to atone for his transgressions, he changed how he treated others and himself. He became grateful for the nursing care he was receiving instead of screaming and yelling. He embraced simple everyday acts of kindness, like saying please and thank you, the words he himself confessed had been missing from his life for many years. He apologized where needed and asked for forgiveness and allowed others to forgive him as he forgave them. He didn't change the world; he just saw it with new eyes; eyes that were not tainted by living in the past or waiting for the future. We talked openly and honestly about the fact that he would soon die, never skirting around the issue. In short, he accepted life just as it was and just as it wasn't. Remember, this was from a man who had spent most of his sixty-seven years in an alcoholic, drug-induced state. He made simple changes; he lived in the moment, and the result was that his last nine days on this earth were spent creating newly loving relationships with his family. In the end, he left our entire family in a place where further healing could occur—this was his gift to us, his legacy. What do you want for your legacy? To die in anger and regret or live for whatever time you have left in peace and love?

SIX

"Love is a state of *being,* not a state of feeling.
That is why when I entered my brother's hospice room in
a space of love, it did not matter what he returned to me."

6

Love

N
ow that we've grounded ourselves in the here and now, it's time to take the next step in this dance of living every moment like we are dying. You will recall that in telling Neil's story, I shared that "I consciously filled my heart with love—love of life, love of death, love of anger, love of hate, love of longing, love of regret, love of disappointment, just *Love*. And then I entered my brother's reality." When I speak of this kind of love—love that is not turned aside by anger, hate, longing, disappointment, regret—I am talking about unconditional love. I know this has become a buzz phrase for many people but let's explore what unconditional love really means.

Most dictionaries define love as "a profoundly tender, deep affection for another person." This kind of love is conditional in that we love that person as long as they return our affection or act in a way that we require. The core of romantic love is based on the premise that some people deserve our love but others do not. It is a feeling; we feel love for a particular person. This kind of love assumes that we will get something in exchange for giving our love. In contrast, unconditional love is not a feeling. It is a state of consciousness, a way of being. I *became* love and then entered my brother's room. I was literally in a state of *being* love, and there was no expectation of anything in return. I loved regardless of whether my love would be reciprocated.

Love has become a four-letter word in our world. Many people use it to gain power and control over another person: "I will love you as long as…" is quite literally a weapon of mass destruction. The word is so misused that it has become hard to discern its true meaning. I have talked to so many people who despise love and the mere mention will send them into a complete tirade because spouses, parents, children and others have wielded the word to motivate them to act in a certain way. The word has been used to take away free will, to manipulate and control, to instill fear of abandonment and guilt.

When I speak of love, however, it comes from a completely different space. Love "is." It can't be easily defined. It is that unconditional feeling of peace and goodwill, and it arises from a place deep within us that calls us to treat everyone and everything with compassion. It is not romantic love, or parental love, or the love that exists between friends. It is just love. It is a calling based on a genuine compassion for life. It exists everywhere and within everything. It is not dependent on the relationship being reciprocated. It is not contingent on our receiving anything in return. It is holding a space filled to overflowing with love.

That is the kind of space I held for my brother. Now trust me, there were moments when he pushed my buttons, times when I had to leave his room to consciously regain that sense of love, that space where I expected nothing of him, but stayed present with him while he ranted and raved. It is so hard to adequately explain, but this kind of love is not changed by external circumstances. Unconditional love allows you to stay in the mindset that everything that is happening is happening in divine right order, and all is as it should be right here and right now. You don't judge it, condemn it, or wish it were different; you accept it for what it is and what it is not. That kind of love is similar to the love an animal gives to its owner. You can ignore a dog but it will always be there in your time of need. No matter how you might treat it, your dog will be there faithfully to lick your wounds. It expects nothing; it loves you in spite of your flaws. Applied to human relationships, that is the space where healing occurs.

It is not easy to get to that space, but it is so essential. With my brother, I stayed in the place of *being* love even when he was yelling at the nurses, telling me go away, not taking his medicine, and sneaking cigarettes. I just held the space until he calmed down and he could begin to feel the love overtake him. Love is the strongest energetic vibration on earth; nothing can defend against it. If we can stay in a place of love, we can move mountains and gentle the raging of ego driven minds.

Love in this sense is not that gushy feeling we have for one another or for things. Unconditional love is the sense that we are a part of something greater than ourselves, oneness with others, and we are happy to be a part of the communion. Our uniqueness in this oneness is all we need and we have no need for others to be different than they are in order to love them. In this kind of love is the knowing that we are supported and guided and protected by something deep within us. Unconditional love connects us to that part of ourselves. It doesn't matter whether you believe in God, a Higher Power, or the energy that connects us all; each and every one of us is part of the whole. We each make up our own little piece of the puzzle of life. Ultimately we all have a voice within us that tells us what to do, when to do it, how to do it, and why to do it. When we make contact with that voice, it creates peace, harmony and a sense of well being like nothing else. This is unconditional love.

Once this level of love is discovered there is nothing we can't do. It is all we need because Love really does conquer all. The easiest and most efficient way to come in contact with this voice inside of you is in the stillness. Take a quiet moment and listen. Listen inwardly. Now you begin to hear a voice. What is it saying? Is it kind? Is it gentle? Is it loving? I must caution you, there is more than one voice inside of you but only one is the voice of Love. This voice will not condemn you nor degrade you but will offer support and encouragement. The other voices will tell you that you are not good enough and you can't do it. Shut them off and listen to the one that says you are awesome; you've got this. Once you tune in to this voice, hold on with all your might. Don't let it go. Stay in that place where love is all there is.

You have now raised your vibrational energy to a place of love. Remember love is a state of *being,* not a state of feeling.

That is why when I entered my brother's hospice room in a space of love, it did not matter what he returned to me. When he presented me with anger, I countered with love. When he yelled, I loved. When he complained, I loved. When he cried, I loved. When he choked, I loved. When he asked for forgiveness, I loved. When he transformed himself, I loved. When he died, I loved. I stayed in a place of absolute love that was not conditioned on what he did or did not do. That love came from within and was sustained by that space deep within me. I strive to live my daily life in this space of love. Am I perfect? No. But with practice, I am pretty good.

You, too, can become pretty good at being loving. You can choose to "feel" love or you can choose to "be" love. It is entirely up to you. I say that from a place of complete non-judgment and absolute love. Both are valid choices and will enhance your life. It is up to you to decide which one will offer you the greatest benefit. It truly is that simple: Choose!

SEVEN

"In order for our loved ones to experience true peace at the end, we must find a way to talk to them about how they view the afterlife or lack thereof, without imposing our own beliefs."

7

After We Die

I felt it necessary to leave this chapter for later in the book as it deals with issues that may be intensely personal to many. But I trust that the previous chapters have more than prepared you to entertain the question of what happens after we die. We talked earlier about accepting others' viewpoints without feeling the need to adopt or change them. This chapter returns to that idea, with a respectful and loving awareness that many of us have extremely strong opinions when it comes to the existence or lack of existence of life after death. I truly believe it does not matter what views you hold; it has no impact on finding the joy in dying. But in order for our loved ones to experience true peace at the end, we must find a way to talk to them about how they view the afterlife or lack thereof, without imposing our own beliefs. Although I, too, have my own beliefs, I will do my best to try to help you understand the importance of complete acceptance of a loved one's particular understanding of what happens when we die, even if that understanding differs from your own. This is not the time to argue semantics. It is a time to foster love and harmony.

For some of you, the idea of allowing a loved one who is dying to hold spiritual beliefs that may be radically different from your own may stretch you far beyond your comfort zone. That being said, your ability to "go there" will absolutely enhance your ability to embrace life, so bear with me, and to the degree you are able, please open your heart. It's worth noting that if you have been diagnosed with a terminal illness for the most part you already have a good grasp on what you think happens after death. I understand that this is not true in every case but most of us do have some ideas. If, however, you do not know how you feel and are not sure what your Truth is, then you need to begin a discussion to help establish where you stand. Where does your body go? Do we have a soul? Will your essence continue on this earth? These are all aspects that need to be explored to determine your Truth—what *you* believe happens after death.

Your Truth is not necessarily your family's Truth, not necessarily your friends', your spouse's, or your children's Truth. It is simply what *you* believe. If you stand in *your* Truth, you can find peace and love in death. I am emphasizing the "you" and the "your" in this scenario because you are the one dying, not your family and friends. This Truth is yours alone and it need not be adopted or validated by others around you, nor does their view need to be adopted by you. Once you determine your view, you can move forward with the dying process. It is important to make this determination because if you can visualize life after death or find comfort in the nonexistence of life after death, it will allow you to die with a greater sense of peace.

Now even though most of us have an idea of what we think happens after death, as we near death, this idea may change. So why am I even including this notion of accepting the belief in an afterlife or in the lack of an afterlife as one of the steps in the dying process? I am trying to help you become familiar with different spiritual viewpoints so you can get clear on what you believe if you are the one facing death, or so that you can help your loved ones find peace at the end of their life by having a conversation with them about what they believe happens after death.

With people who believe in life after death, talk about how that life will look. Get specific. Do they believe in heaven and hell? What do these places look like? Do they believe their soul lives on? Do they believe they will come back again in a new incarnation? Do they think they will see their loved ones who have already passed away? What do they think they will look like in the afterlife? Keep asking questions so the dying person can get a clear picture of his or her idea of what life after death will be like. In my brother's case, he said he would become young and vibrant again when he passed. He would no longer be sick, weak, or gray. He felt that he would look like he did in his forties. Once he had a clear view of where he was going and what it was going to look like there, all fear left him. At the end, he was able to take his oxygen off while declaring, "This is just delaying the inevitable." He passed within twelve hours of that declaration. That is the kind of peace I am talking about. Regardless of whether you agreed with Neil's viewpoint, he passed in peace.

For me there was an additional bonus because when my brother died, I was left with seeing him in that light instead of as a frail sick man railing at the fates. I had a clear view that he trusted where he was going and that he felt it was to a place of love. When I think of Neil now, I see him as this forty-year-old who is singing with Elvis in heaven. I feel the essence of him each day as I write this book. His presence is still here because I am still here and his essence will be present with me and for me as long as I live.

The essence of those who have passed away is present whether you are Christian, Atheist, Metaphysical, Spiritual, Agnostic or any other belief system. Let me explain. I am sure each of you can recall a deceased relative or friend. Now if you stop for a moment you will feel their essence right here and now. You can still see this person in your mind's eye, can still hear their laughter ringing in your memory, can still feel what it was like to be in their presence when they were on earth. That's what I am talking about when I refer to their essence.

The conversation about what happens when we die is a beautiful gift for all who participate in it. It brings peace to the dying process. It brings acceptance and joy to dying. It allows you to share and refine your own views of death and life after death. Once you get a clear picture of how you see the dying process, it enables you to accept your own mortality, and the fact that someday everyone who is alive will be in this position of facing death. And lastly this conversation will help those left behind to survive the grief of losing your physical being from their life.

For those who do not believe in life after death, it is just as important to discuss what they believe happens to their essence after they die. What is important to them? What are their concerns about dying? Is there anything they need to accomplish before they pass that will allow their energy a smooth transition from their body? What is required to help them pass with peace and love? Again, just open the discussion, and listen with acceptance.

Someone very close to me is an Atheist and he says what would be important to him on his deathbed is the legacy he is leaving behind. He says it would be important for him to know that his energy will be present in the lives of his loving wife, his children, and his other family members. Everyone wants the same thing, remember. We all want to leave the world better than we found it and we want to know that we added peace and love to this world. It doesn't matter what your view is, it is important to share it with your loved ones. Don't take precious time trying to convince them that you are right or wrong, just stand in your own Truth. Stay true to what you believe but at the same time allow them to stay in their Truth. We do not need to convince others of our Truth, we just need to express it and put words to it so we can die in peace.

This conversation about what we believe happens when we die can benefit us at any stage of life, whether we are in good health or are aged and near the end of life. For example, my editor called me one day to talk about this book but instead our conversation turned to her mother, who was ninety-two and very frail. Her mother had been praying for death, but my editor felt ambivalent, not wanting to lose physical contact with her beloved mother. I told her two things. First, she needed to give her mother permission to die and to be open to it as a possible choice her mother might make in the near future. We don't have to fight to extend our life. There is a distinction between fighting to live and fighting to stay alive. Her mother's condition was such that she was fighting to stay alive. Her body was worn out and she felt she had no true purpose in living anymore. By giving our loved ones permission to die, we allow people the right to make guilt-free choices for themselves when their bodies are giving out and they no longer have any quality of life. Many times our family members are holding on because we can't let them go and they don't want to disappoint us. But there is no shame in saying my body and mind have had all they can take. It is time for me to go. By making this clear choice we can move on to the next step and that is the visualization of what comes after death.

My second piece of advice to my editor was for her to talk to her mom openly about dying, and to ask her clearly and without judgment what did she envision would happen to her after death? My editor learned that her mother felt that she would be reunited with loved ones who had passed earlier, and that she was going to heaven. She looked forward to seeing her husband again, and her parents who had been gone so long. My editor felt a sense of calm settle over her time with her mother as they talked in this way, and her anxiety about her mother's passing began to recede.

In any situation with a loved one who is near death, just begin a casual conversation about dying. It is not something to avoid. This conversation eliminates any negativity about death. We are all going to die and leave this world; why do we make it such a horrible thing? Dying is a part of life, an amazing and inevitable part of a life that has been completely lived.

EIGHT

"We as humans are in constant search for meaning. We are seeking the answers to the eternal questions: Why am I here? What do I want from life? What will give my life purpose? How can I be happy? How do I find peace?"

8

My Transformation

I have walked you through many lessons that will help bring you joy in dying. In all truth, I could stop at this point but I am compelled to delve deeper. If you are still reading then you are ready to hear the rest of my story. It explains how I also became a facilitator to the healing process and how I personally found the space where I could discover the joy in dying. I believe that we all have the ability to heal ourselves; we just need a guide. As a metaphysician who counsels individuals on healing the mind, the body, and the soul, I have accepted the task of being that trusted guide, the person who is willing to join others on their journey towards self-discovery and wellness. I truly am grateful to be able to do this work, and I completely embrace the fact that I was put on this great wonderful planet to help heal the world. I have been given no greater gift than to be charged with that duty and I accept it with an open heart.

You may find it curious that my healing work should also include helping people die with joy and peace. It is actually not so odd, because when our time on this earth is winding down, we cannot put off any longer taking the steps that will allow us to heal our relationships with others and finally embrace our life in all its fullness and glory. In this way I am a healer of not just the physical body but also of the emotional and spiritual body. To the core of my being, I believe we are responsible for what is in our life and that the choices we make are affected by our past. We allow the past to create limitations for us that hinder us from living our fullest lives. I further understand that once we utilize the amazing power of choice, we become truly alive and develop an authentic sense of who we are; we become self-aware. We also encounter the very uncomfortable knowledge that it is in our hands to live rich and satisfying lives. This can be very unnerving to some people. They face the dilemma that opening doors to new worlds closes doors to the old world. They must begin to embrace a new way of thinking of the past, the present, and the future. This can cause a great deal of conflict but with the right information and with a trusted guide to hold their hand, all people can learn to embrace this sense of responsibility and live full and complete lives.

My choice to become a healer began many years ago. I was called into this, I guess you may call it a profession, but I see it more as a "state of being." I don't recall the moment it happened; I just remember one morning I awoke and realized that I needed to help people reach their full potential; to be the catalyst that jolted them into identifying and achieving the goals that would serve their highest purpose. Initially, I was called to begin working on my master's degree and had every intention of becoming a licensed professional counselor. I finished all the course work for the program and began to contemplate where I would complete my internship and residency when I had the strong realization that counseling was not the calling. How crazy is that? I had spent several years and many thousands of dollars to discover that, no, this was not the stopping point. I struggled with that idea for a few months, wavering between finishing my degree and exploring the unknown.

The unknown won and thus began my journey. I began to travel to various places, taking courses on how to become more self-aware. I took seminars that opened my mind to the endless possibilities available for my life. Each journey moved me farther along the path and further supported the knowing that counseling was not my calling. My true calling is to teach people how to connect with their own inner knowing and to awaken the "Truth" of who they are that is locked within them. I want to reach that place deep inside them; that place that counseling alone cannot touch; the place that knows what is required to find true peace and tranquility in life; the place that can only be reached by contemplation and meditation; the place that holds all that is important to them as individuals.

My own journey opened up this feeling in me, this overwhelming concern for humanity, a sense that we were missing something in the story of our lives. I just knew there was more to our life than work and play. Was there a deeper meaning and purpose for each of us to discover and if so what was it? My first step, of course, was to examine and change my own beliefs and values and develop a strong sense of self-knowing and self-love. I began this self-discovery with tools that I learned during my counseling education. It was during this process that I discovered and embraced the premise that we as humans are in a constant search for meaning. We are seeking the answers to the eternal questions: Why am I here? What do I want from life? What will give my life purpose? How can I be happy? How do I find peace?

As the answers to these questions began to unfold for me, I realized I was being divinely guided. I would hear of one self-awareness retreat or another, and soon I began to attend them. Each would offer a different insight into how to reach inside oneself and how to truly discover what mattered most to me, not what mattered to my family or my friends, but what mattered to *me*. I opened my mind and soul to all the possibilities that were available in my life. As I explored the areas within myself where I was holding onto old wounds, hurts and resentments, I began to discover that past was in complete control. Not only had it molded my belief system, but also it was completely dominant in my current life. Those past wounds were keeping me from experiencing all the beauty life had to offer me in the here and now. I quickly, well maybe not so quickly, recognized that all these old wounds were preventing me from living my life to the fullest each and every day.

Little by little, as I attended various retreats and seminars, I began to embrace two very important concepts: living in the here and now and learning and mastering the act of forgiveness. I started to view my life differently. I realized that much of my day was either spent worrying about things I had done in the past or wondering what the future would hold for me. I would continually beat myself up over trivial comments made to others or because of mistakes I had made in relationships. It seemed like a good portion of my time was taken over by the past but not all of it—there was also the time that I spent contemplating how much better my life would be in the future.

Oh yes, that amazing future in which everything will be much better. The time when that magical event occurs that will make all our dreams come true; we will win the lottery, we will find our perfect match, we will make peace with our parents and family, we will resolve our financial issues. There is always that pie in the sky; we just know we will reach it tomorrow. Now I am not saying there is anything wrong with envisioning your future and setting goals, but many of us become obsessed with that time and until that time arrives we are just putting up with life; existing at best. What I discovered through my journey is that this does not serve our higher purpose. What if we could have that amazing life right here, right now, with exactly what we already have?

I set myself on a course of enjoying life as it was, not as I wanted it to be. I soon began to realize that by accepting my reality in the here and now, I was finally beginning to experience exactly what I wanted all along. I was discovering peace and tranquility and love. Now firmly grounded in the here and now, I began the next leg of my journey, learning the act of forgiveness.

I started forgiving everyone; I forgave my mother and father for all I thought they had done wrong; I forgave my family and my friends; I forgave my co-workers and former co-workers; I forgave my childhood friends, and basically anyone else I felt had hurt me in the past. I was even able to forgive people who had passed away and those who were no longer in my life. Initially it was a tedious process, but soon I began to experience an elevated level of freedom so I forgave more and more and more. With each act I felt peace and calm overtake my body. It was as if I had lost half my body weight. Wow, this feeling was almost like a drug, but as all drugs do it began to lose its effectiveness. There must be something else, I thought. I felt a sense of peace and tranquility but there was still this empty space inside of me. Something was still causing me moments of strife and anxiety. What was I missing?

The answer, as always, came in the right order and at the right time. If I have learned nothing else through this journey it is to ask the question then to sit quietly back and allow the answer to be revealed. The answer came when one of my trusted life guides suggested meditation to calm my anxiety. During my daily meditation, I discovered the answer I had been seeking right there inside of myself. Through all that work, I had forgotten to forgive the most important person in my life—myself. Oh, this is going to be rough, I remember thinking. I recalled that when I first started forgiving others, I had struggled so much. It didn't take long before I understood that as difficult as it was to forgive others, it was nothing in comparison to what I faced in trying to forgive myself.

This was one of the most difficult steps for me during this process, to accept that I had any part in the issue. I had this attitude of: He cheated on me, she hurt my feelings when she called me ugly, they had no right to quit talking to me, and my Mom should never have done that to me. What did I do "wrong?" I was just the innocent bystander. I argued that point with myself for a good long time and then I realized that whether I was the "perpetrator" or the "victim" (I use these terms not because I necessarily believe in them but because of the universal understanding of their meanings), there was something to forgive. But what was it? I knew in order to truly reach my full potential, I had to forgive myself, but for what? It eventually became apparent that for every wrong I felt others had done to me, I had attached a meaning about myself that I had to forgive. For instance, if someone disliked me then I attached the meaning that I was unlikeable and I had to forgive myself for thinking I was unlikeable. If someone got angry with me or was disappointed in me, I attached a meaning that I was not worthy and I needed to forgive myself for feeling unworthy.

The more I forgave myself the more love I began to develop for this human being named T. The more I saw my own worth and removed the tainted lenses of other people's opinions of who I was, the more I understood that I was just a human being doing the best I could with what I had, and that opened to the door to me forgiving myself for the times when I wasn't who I wanted to be. It was that simple in the end. Now, each time I feel myself slipping back into my old ways, I learn the lesson anew: I forgive myself for anything I feel I did wrong, and then simply move forward.

You will learn as you move through this process that forgiveness has little to do with the other person or with the event that caused the strife in the first place. Instead it is a gift one gives to oneself. Remember, you simply replace the words "I forgive" with "for I give"—for I give myself love.

My next step—I would say my last step but this act of fully experiencing life is an ongoing process—was to begin working on reaching my inner self, that place inside me that holds all the answers to the questions of life. This step was facilitated through meditation. There are many ways to learn the art of meditation. Countless books have been written on the subject; one can attend guided meditation workshops or various religious organizations offer guidance in this area. Regardless of how the knowledge is acquired, the process of meditation offers you a method of really reaching that deep internal knowing we all possess—the place where you "know" what you need and want in your life; the place where the True Self lives. Once you establish the connection with your indwelling spirit, you will see your life start to fall into place. It may not be in perfect harmony all at once, but you will feel the struggle and anxiety begin to diminish.

My life has been much like a roller coaster ride. I have had some amazing highs and some extremely scary lows but all in all I have really enjoyed the ride and look forward to the many twists and turns that remain to be encountered. Through much hard work, I have started the process of enlightenment and have set my life in forward motion, embracing the infinite possibilities that are available to me. I am not saying that I have discovered all the definitive answers to life's great questions, as they are different for each of us, but I have discovered a way that will help each person answer them for themselves.

In addition to the work that I have completed on my own, the story of my transformation and perspective on life would not be complete without talking about my father's influence. My father taught me to be strong, opinionated, and hardworking. When he was diagnosed with lung cancer in 2005, seven years before my brother Neil's diagnosis, I was fortunate enough to be able to spend his last four months caring for him and extracting the last bits of wisdom from him. My experience of my father's death was a major reason for writing this book, but in a way that was much different than Neil's death. My lack of training and wisdom during my dad's dying process still causes me to pause. I did not possess the same level of knowledge during his passing as I did with Neil's. As a result, my father's death was far more traumatic for him and my family than my brother's. I did not have the understanding that would have allowed me to help my father in his hour of need, but I can aid other dying people and their families to find not only peace in death but also joy. This book is a way for me to realize my dream of being a catalyst to help other people reach their full potential. I want to make the world a better place to live and die.

NINE

"Oh, what a different picture we create when rather than fighting death and trying to stay alive, we embrace the dying process and *truly live* for whatever time we have left."

9

My Father's Story

There was a stark contrast between my dad's passing and my brother's. My brother, although he lived a life filled with anger and frustration, died a death filled with peace and love. My father on the other hand lived a life filled with peace and love but died a death filled with fear and anxiety. I hope that sharing the details of his passing will help each of you embrace the ideas I have outlined in this book as you embark on your own journey to finding the joy in dying.

I will begin this chapter by simply stating that my father was the most amazing human being I have ever been blessed to know. He was one of kind, and to have him as my daddy was one of my life's richest gifts. When he was thirty-four years old, having been a professed bachelor, he married my Mom. She was a single mother of nine, yes nine children. My dad, who was a mechanical equipment operator and jack-of-all-trades, became an instant father to all of them. To everyone's surprise, he and my mother went on to have two more children, my sister and me.

As a young girl I remember tagging along with my dad on his daily chores and pitching in wherever I could. Throughout my life he was my confidante and friend. We spent hours talking politics, religion, life, boyfriends, kids, current events, and any other subject that happened to come to us. As a child I was inseparable from him. He was my strength and my rock in times of struggle and I could always count on him for support and sound advice. So when he was diagnosed with lung cancer it felt like one of my vital organs was being ripped from me. I couldn't imagine life without him. How could I possibly exist without this extraordinary man?

I know most people who have lost a loved one can relate to this feeling. We begin with the thought *no way can they die*. Fear grips us to the core of everything we are and we immediately begin to deny the inevitable, knowing that somehow there will be some miracle and our loved one will live. My father's death story was no different.

My dad immediately began receiving radiation treatments to stunt the growth of the tumor, which merely extended his life from a month to seven months. He became extremely ill and fragile. He even lost his cognitive skills during this treatment but he fought for every bit of life he could get. He had little energy to function in his daily life and this man who had worked fifteen hours a day could barely find the energy to make it to his radiation treatments, each of which was followed by extended periods of sleep and sickness. He continued to take the treatments, believing they would actually make him better, so he would not pass away. The small precious amount of time left in his life was spent hoping and praying for a miracle, but the miracle didn't come.

He became weaker and weaker as cancer patients do, and he began to come to grips with the fact that he was dying. He soon expressed to the doctors that he was ready to stop treatments and that he could tell his passing was inevitable; this information was never verbalized to any of us in the family, however. In retrospect, I wonder if he felt we would have viewed him as a quitter, and sadly I must confess we may have. Our own fear of living without him would probably have clouded our view and we would have begged him to continue fighting. As it was, the doctor's had extended his radiation far longer than needed because they were waiting for him to accept his death. This caused a great deal of damage and in the end his death was riddled with many extra complications and a great deal of agonizing pain. He went through things that no human being should ever experience. As I write these words, tears well in my eyes thinking of the great fight that he endured just so his little girl wouldn't lose her Daddy, her confidante, her rock. So his family wouldn't lose the glue that held them all together and repaired all their wounds. So his wife wouldn't lose the love of her life.

He became weaker and weaker as the weeks went by and we soon moved him into my sister's house, where she could help my mother care for him. I eventually moved in with them and helped care for him during the last part of his life. I don't want to make this sound like a burden because truly it was not.

Even in his altered state he had little bits of wisdom that he was able to bestow.

We did what most families do. We gathered around him, praising him for all he had been to us and thanking him for blessing our lives with his presence. And he reacted as most dying people do, explaining how he had not been there enough, he hadn't accomplished what he thought he should have, he hadn't been a good enough husband, father, or grandfather. Expressing all the regrets of a lifetime; apologizing for everything that he felt he hadn't given his family. We all tried to express what an amazing person he was and to thank him for the love and grace he had shown to us even during this time of sickness, but he couldn't hear the words. He smiled that same boyish grin that had been his signature smile for as long as I can remember, but under the smile lingered the sense of regret. In the end, I think it was this same feeling of regret that caused him to labor for every breath, holding on to this life and this body for all he had, gasping for every breath in hopes that somehow he could change the past; try again; be the man he wanted to be.

I would like you each to understand that in spite of my lack of knowledge of the joy in dying, there were moments of bliss and memories that were created during my father's final days that I will cherish forever. I was so grateful to be a witness to his dying experience, thankful for the opportunity to stand beside him. But death truly is a one-man job. We can ride along for part of the journey but the dying person must finally be the sole passenger on the train. That being said, we can find beauty and joy in the process. This dying time is a creative time and somewhere along the way, we humans have forgotten that. We have made the dying process "bad," therefore we no longer are able to see this time for what it truly is—a time to build, to create, to love, to find joy, to be in the presence of greatness, and to receive the reward for a life well lived.

Now mind you, I am not saying there is anything "wrong" with how my family went through this process, but in retrospect I look at all the time spent regretting a past that could not be changed and envisioning a future that would never be lived. I wonder if we had stayed present in that moment, in the here and now, how different the scene would look. Would the struggle have been less, would the regrets have been lessened and would my beloved father have been able to hear the words of praise that his family bestowed upon him? The answer of course is maybe.

I cannot change the past, nor am I trying to. Everything with my father's death happened as it was meant to, but I use his example hopefully to explain my new frame of reference: My goal now is to help others pass with a greater sense of peace and joy; to use this dying time as a time for healing, not only for the dying person but for the family as a whole; to create a space for forgiveness, for love. If I knew then what I know now, instead of focusing on how I was going to live without my father in my life, I would have focused on how I was going to help him live his last days to their fullest. I would instantly begin helping him clean up the past so he could become present in the moment. So he could learn to live in the right here, right now. So he could accept the situation as it was; so he could freely choose to quit fighting to stay alive.

When we fight to stay alive, as opposed to fighting to live, we are just struggling to keep from dying. We are doing everything we can to ward off death. As long as our bodies are breathing, we think that is what matters regardless of whether we are hooked up to a machine or strapped to a bed unable to speak. This is not living.

Now let's look at what it means to fight to live. That is a powerful statement, fighting to live. In contrast to fighting to stay alive, fighting to live means making the most of the time we have left. It is the process of becoming present in the here and now, forgiving past indiscretions and hurts, and releasing thoughts of the future that may never be. During this process, we simply are *being;* we are moving forward, creating the life we want regardless of how long we get to live that life.

When we are operating from this point of view, we take our treatments not to extend our life but to give us the opportunity to *live.* We use the time to create new experiences with our family, our loved ones, and our friends. We spend very little time regretting the past, exchanging that time for forgiving past hurts so we can create new memories. Rather than discuss regrets of a life not lived, for instance, my father would have let go of the life he didn't live and exchanged it for the life he had left. He would have forgiven himself for everything he thought he had not managed to do, which would have freed him to fully embrace the last seven months of his life. His view would not have been clouded by regrets but rather he would focus on creating the life he always wanted, finding peace and love in the moment. He would have been able to embrace the last of life with open arms and he would have heard the words of praise and gratitude and love from his family. Oh, what a different picture we create when rather than fighting death and trying to stay alive, we embrace the dying process and *truly live* for whatever time we have left.

TEN

"We are going to leave this world and cease to exist in the physical bodies we currently inhabit. Our essence will remain in the hearts and lives of all who knew us but we will be gone from here. In contemplating that truth, death should not be the fear. Living a life that was less than we wanted and deserved should be the fear. The goal, then, is to ensure that we live a life worth dying for."

10

Joy in Living

Generally, this final chapter would be where everything is all tied up in a nice package and all the points I have made would be reiterated. We'll get to that, but first I have a little bit of a twist to this particular story. Before tying up all the loose ends, I am going to unravel them all. I have been talking about dying throughout this book, which would leave one believing that the book is actually about dying. Quite the contrary, this book is one hundred percent about living. Yes, you are reading it right, because with every step toward finding the joy in dying, I have been directing you to the true premise and goal of this book—to learn to *live* like you are dying. I want each of you who read this book to live every moment of your life as if it is one of your last. I want you to love, forgive, and accept like you will never get another opportunity. I want you to discover the unbelievable peace that comes with living like each moment is precious and time is finite, because in this human form, it is. Everything I have covered in this book will actually help you embrace life to the fullest so that when your time comes to die, you can go in peace. So whether or not you have not been given a terminal diagnosis, let's recap how the steps toward dying with joy can help you live with joy.

I began by telling you the story of my brother's death, but if you carefully read over the chapter you will see I was really telling you about my brother's last days of life. I showed you how we worked through the steps and the amazing life he was able to live; who cares that it was for only nine days? In those last nine days he forged loving relationships and experienced the greatest sense of peace that had ever felt in his entire life. He was able to live life to the fullest for the first time. He was able to do what we all come to this earth to do and that is to create love and peace.

Now let me further explain how this process works to help you live life like you are dying. In the chapter on acceptance, I asked you to accept the situation in which you find yourself exactly as it is. For anyone who has been diagnosed with a terminal illness that means you need to accept that you are dying. But everyone else also needs to accept this eventuality, because every person alive is also dying. I know this can be unsettling but take a moment, right here and now, and just entertain the idea. Don't make it a big deal; most likely you're not going to die in this minute. I mean, you could, but let's assume it's not going to happen right now. But someday, somewhere along the way, you are going to die. It is part of life just like breathing and eating. We will die. It is nothing to fear, nothing to worry about; it is just going to happen. We are going to leave this world and cease to exist in the physical bodies we currently inhabit. Our essence will remain in the hearts and lives of all who knew us but we will be gone from here. In contemplating that truth, death should not be the fear. Living a life that was less than we wanted and deserved should be the fear.

The goal, then, is to ensure that we live a life worth dying for. The first step is the hardest, admitting we are dying. The next step is to begin to *live* like we are dying. The gateway to that expansive and freely loving experience is forgiveness. I know when I started on this path I wanted to clean up past events that were preventing me from living to my fullest. I was on a forgiveness free-for-all, and the more I forgave the more alive I became. People began to notice and they would ask if I had started having Botox treatments because the wrinkles were lessening on my face and I was literally looking and feeling younger. Forgiving literally lifts the weight off of you; if you struggle with your weight and can't seem to let it go, try forgiving yourself and see what happens. It is unbelievable what happens when you begin to forgive. I have worked with so many people to help them forgive. They have left my office saying they felt physically lighter. One woman said she looked in the mirror when she got home and could see that she had fewer wrinkles on her face. Another said it was like having the Empire State building lifted from her chest. Forgiveness is such a healing process. I can't emphasize enough how this will transform your life.

And don't forget to forgive yourself. It is actually the most important step yet it is often neglected. For every person you forgive, you must forgive yourself too, because I can guarantee you are negatively judging yourself in some way based on the resentment you held against that person or event. I know it is difficult, but please don't skip past this part. If you need help, find a therapist or spiritual counselor to work with you to complete this step. In order to live like you are dying—by which I mean to live fully and completely—you must forgive yourself for not living that way up to this point in your life.

Once you begin forgiving other people and yourself, a strange phenomenon happens. You feel yourself living in the present. You no longer spend much time living in the past and very little time regretting things you did or did not do. You begin to notice that you no longer feel shame, you have far less anger, and the moments of hurt are shorter than before. You realize that nothing matters more than this moment; you begin to become present.

The biggest obstacle to maintaining this presence is getting caught up in the "what ifs" and the "buts." You know what I am talking about—*What if I had acted differently, would he have left me?... But my Mom was mean to me.... If I had taken the car keys, would they still be alive?... If I get skinny, then will she love me?*—I think you get my meaning here. Every one of those statements either keeps you locked in the past or looking towards a future that doesn't exist. Let them go; eliminate the "ifs" and "buts" from your vocabulary. I was as guilty as any for being caught up in the "what ifs" and the "buts." I let them go. I now understand I can't change what happened in the past any more than I can't guarantee what will happen in the future; the only place I can make any impact is in the here and now. To become present, you forgive the past, you trust the future, and you live in the moment.

The best advice that I can give for becoming present in the moment is to literally embrace each moment just as it shows up. When I did this, I learned to revel in the simple things: I would pay attention to the moment without judging it. I would look my lover in eyes and literally feel his presence, allowing my body and my mind to embrace that second, that moment we connected. I would feel the water on my feet when I walked on the beach, noticing if it was cold or warm but not judging it, just noticing. When my brother was yelling at me because he was scared, I embraced him just as he was showing up. I didn't wish he were different. I just took the moment for what it was; two people sharing space. When my brother spoke the words, "You need to go so I can go," I let myself feel the sorrow of losing him. I did not judge it; I just let the emotion rush through me for I knew this would be the last time I would be in his physical presence.

Allow yourself to feel and fully experience each moment. Don't lessen it by trying to make it something it is not or wishing it could be different. We only have now and unless we can find a way to be at peace right here and right now, we will never be happy. It's all we are guaranteed; there is no guarantee of tomorrow. If doesn't matter if you are rich or poor, thin or fat, old or young, male or female, or gay or straight. It just is what it is and it cannot be what it is not. Accept it just as it is showing up and you will see your life literally transform before your eyes. I promise that once you accept life just as it is and just as it is not, the struggle ends.

Once the struggle ends, transformation becomes possible. You now have the energy to make positive changes in your life because you are no longer spending all of your energy wishing that your life was somehow different; wishing you had a different job, a different family, a different body, a different spouse, a different child, a different something. Now you can use that energy to find what will fulfill you. Live in the now and you may even discover that this job, family, body, spouse, child are exactly what you need. You never know what will show up for you in the present. You may find yourself in a hospice room helping someone you haven't spoken to in twenty years pass away and it may be the single event that changes your life forever. Go with the flow, live in the moment, and your life will never be the same. In short, live like there is no tomorrow!

So where to go from here? You have accepted your own mortality, you have forgiven everyone you know, and you are living in the here and now. What else is there to do? Oh yeah, there is that thing called love—that four-letter word that brings so many emotions to the forefront. For some it evokes warm feelings, for some frustration, for some loneliness, for some anger, and for some happiness. The word Love has been so misused in our society: We love everything from ice cream, to movies, to sex, and yes even other humans as long as they are acting the way we want them to. We have to somehow redefine that word; we have to take it back to the true meaning and its purest and unconditional sense.

Love is not a mechanism to control other people, though many of us have been guilty of using it that way. Love is not a tool to get your own way. Love is not a feeling. It is not learned. Love just is. You have to *become* love. This kind of unconditional love is a state of consciousness. You literally *are* love; it is inherent in your soul to *be* love. When we are babies we love in the purest sense, but we are soon conditioned by our society to only give love if certain conditions exist, like being loved in return.

I became love in my brother's hospice room; the conditions should have made me angry or hurt but I stayed in the state of being love and it melted his heart. There is no defense against unconditional love; it will end all conflict if you can just stay in that space. Now I am not saying it is easy to stay in that space, it takes connecting to that inner self through consistent practice to stay in that space. There were times that I would have to leave my brother's room and reconnect to that place inside of me, where nothing exists but love. Spend time in daily meditation and you will be able to stay in connection with that inner you, with the love inside of you. What I am challenging you to do now and from this day forth is to just *be* love. Love conquers all fear, drives out all hate, anger, hurt and despair. Love is the strongest emotion there is and the whole source of our ability to live a wholly fulfilling life. Whether you are facing a time of trial or a time of calm, nothing can destroy you, not even death, when your very essence is love.

Now you have the tools to do what I hope this book has inspired in you:

Live each moment like you're dying—*because you are!*

About the Author

T is the mother of two amazing children, a son and daughter, both who have blessed her life with their presence and love. She has had many professions in this life, each one bringing her a step closer to fulfilling her true passion which is to help alleviate the suffering in people's lives and help them experience peace and love. T holds a Ph.D. in Philosophy specializing in Holistic Life Counseling. Such a long name to describe what she does, which is help people identify the emotional wounds in their lives and help them heal those wounds. It is with a humble heart that she offers to guide them through their own healing work, for after all each person, alone, must complete the healing process. No one can do it for them. So in following through with that goal she offers these words to help guide people along their path.

Printed in the United States
By Bookmasters